WAFFLE IT WITH THIS AMAZING BELGIAN WAFFLE COOKBOOK: WAFFLES SO FLUFFY, LIGHT, AND DELICIOUS!

First edition. September 15, 2021.

Copyright © 2021 Ida Smith.

ISBN: 979-8201688080

Written by Ida Smith.

Table of Contents

Waffle It with this Amazing Belgian Waffle Cookbook

Waffles So Fluffy, Light, and Delicious!

BY: Ida Smith

License Notes

This book is licensed for your personal enjoyment only. This book may not be re-sold or given away to other people. If you would like to share this book with another person, please purchase an additional copy for each recipient. If you're reading this book and did not purchase it, or it was not purchased for your use only, then please return to your favorite ebook retailer and purchase your own copy. Thank you for respecting the hard work of this author.

Introduction

Before we go further into this Belgian waffle cookbook, let's quickly share some interesting facts about waffles!

The first waffle recipe was found in the 14th century in the Le Ménagier de Paris manuscript.

The most popular waffle recipes in the world are American, Hong Kong, Dutch, and, of course, Belgian!

Patrick Bertoletti ate the most record in 10 minutes. He ate 29 waffles in 10 minutes!?

Someone sang a song for waffles!? Parry Gripp did sing a song for waffles titled "Do You Like Waffles?"

Of course!! We all love waffles, and that's why, you are here to learn more ways that you can enjoy them.

And not to disappoint you, this Belgian waffles cookbook will show you new and interesting ways to cook waffles!! Enjoy!!

1. Belgian Waffle

Yes, there is a Belgian waffle that is not a dish. Alas, it's a drink!!!

Prep time: 05 minutes
Cooking time: nil
Servings: 1
Ingredients

- 1 oz Belgian ale
- 1 oz Guinness stout

Directions
Pour the ale up to half of a beer mug.
Fill the remaining half with the stout; pour over a spoon.
Serve.

2. Black Belgian Waffle

You have been seeing lots of golden brown waffles everywhere, but Belgians decided to switch things up, and we are loving this black waffle version!!

Prep time: 15 minutes
Cooking time: 25 minutes
Servings: 12
Ingredients

- 4 eggs (separated)
- 100ml distilled cherry water
- 400g whole wheat flour
- 100g dark sugar
- 100g cocoa powder
- 1 teaspoon yeast
- 500ml milk
- 150g butter
- 200g cherries (pitted and halved)
- 3 tablespoons whipped cream
- 200g dark chocolate

Directions
Melt the chocolate, yeast, sugar, and butter in a pan.
Mix well to dissolve the sugar properly.

Combine the cocoa powder, egg yolks, and flour in a bowl. Mix well.
Whisk the egg whites in another bowl till stiff peaks form.
Add the sugar mixture into the flour mixture. Mix well.
Add the distilled cherry water, milk, and egg white. Mix well.
Spoon the batter into the iron. Cook till the batter is exhausted.
Serve the waffles warm and garnish with the cherries and whipped cream.
Enjoy.

3. Banana Twist Belgian Waffle

Do you want to treat your partner to a perfect breakfast in bed with waffles? This is the perfect waffle recipe designed for lovers!!

Prep time: 10 minutes
Cooking time: 14 minutes
Servings: 2
Ingredients

- 1 cup butter (melted)
- 1 teaspoon baking soda
- 1 tablespoon vanilla extract
- 1 cup milk
- 1 cup flour
- 1 pinch salt
- 3 teaspoons sugar
- 2 large eggs
- 1 ripe banana (mashed)
- 1 cup gelato
- 1 cup dark chocolate (melted)

Directions

Preheat and grease your waffle iron.

Combine the dry ingredients in a bowl. Mix well.

Mix the butter, banana, vanilla extract, milk, and eggs in another bowl. Whisk well.
Gradually stir in the dry ingredients.
Mix well.
Spoon the batter on the waffle iron. Cook till done.
Cook till the entire batter is exhausted.
Transfer the waffles to plates.
Serve immediately with the gelato and melted chocolate.

4. Red Velvet Belgian Waffles

Not a red velvet cake!!

Prep time: 15 minutes

Cooking time: 40 minutes

Servings: 12

Ingredients

- 8 eggs
- 2 (30 oz) boxes red velvet cake mix
- 8 tablespoons soft cream cheese
- 1 cup mini chocolate chips
- 4 cups powdered sugar
- 5 cups milk

Directions

Preheat your waffle maker.

Combine the 4 cups of the milk, the cake mix, and eggs in a bowl. Mix till fully combined.

In another bowl, combine the remaining milk, cream cheese, and sugar. Mix well.

Spray the waffle maker with cooking spray.

Scoop the batter into the waffle maker. Cook till done.

Cook till you have exhausted your batter.

Serve the waffles. Garnish with a drizzling of the cream cheese mixture and chocolate chips.

Enjoy.

5. Keto Belgian Waffle

As someone on a keto diet, you may want to enjoy waffles regardless of your diet type, but you don't want to risk your luck with carbs!!

Here is the solution!! The perfect Belgian waffle recipe for a keto diet!!

Prep time: 04 minutes
Cooking time: 05 minutes
Servings: 2
Ingredients

- 1 pinch baking powder
- 3 tablespoons coconut flour
- 1 teaspoon maple flavor
- 4 oz soft cream cheese
- 3 large eggs
- 1 tablespoon monk fruit sweetener
- 1 pinch xanthan gum
- 1 pinch cinnamon powder

Directions
Preheat the iron. Put the coconut flour in the food processor.
Add the cream cheese and maple flavor next. Add the eggs, baking powder, sweetener, and gum. Blitz thoroughly.
Spray the iron with non-stick cooking spray.

Scoop the processed mixture on the iron.
Cook till you're done with the batter.
Transfer the cooked waffles to a plate.
Serve and add a drizzle of the cinnamon powder.

6. Belgian Waffle Bliss and Confetti

Let's start our Belgian waffle cookbook with this amazing recipe that deserves to be enjoyed in bliss!!

Prep time: 04 minutes

Cooking time: 16 minutes

Servings: 6

Ingredients

- 6 tablespoons milk
- 9 tablespoons flour
- 1 medium egg (separated your egg white and yolk)
- 1 tablespoon granulated sugar
- 1 teaspoon vanilla extract
- 1 tablespoon canola oil
- 1 pinch salt
- 1 teaspoon baking powder
- 1 tablespoon butter

Directions

Preheat the waffle iron to 260 degrees F.

Beat the egg white in a bowl till it forms a stiff peak.

Combine the butter, milk, vanilla extract, oil, and egg yolk in another bowl. Mix well.

Combine the salt, flour, baking powder, and sugar in another bowl. Mix well.

Slowly mix the dry ingredients into the bowl of the wet ingredients. Mix well. Add the egg white.

Brush your waffle iron grids with butter.

Pour the mixture into the bottom grid.

Shut the iron.

Cook till done.

Do this till the mixture is exhausted.

Serve the waffles warm.

Enjoy.

7. Belgian Waffles Pops

What a perfect Belgian waffle recipe to round off our cookbook!!

Prep time: 20 minutes
Cooking time: 13 minutes
Servings: 3
Ingredients

- 1 tablespoon peanut butter chips (chopped)
- 1 tablespoon almonds (sliced)
- 2 readymade chilled chocolate waffles
- 2 readymade chilled buttermilk waffles
- 3 tablespoons milk chocolate chips (melted)
- 1 tablespoon rainbow sprinkles
- 3 tablespoons butterscotch chips (melted)
- 1 tablespoon mini chocolate chips

Directions
Cut the two corners of each waffle so that they can have pointed ends.
Place them on a paper lined baking sheet.
Pour the melted chocolate into a Ziploc bag.
Pour the melted butterscotch into another Ziploc bag.

Cut the tips of the bags and drizzle the chocolate first over your waffles, followed by a drizzling of the butterscotch on the chocolate.

Sprinkle the rainbow sprinkles and almonds over the chocolate and butterscotch.

Top with the peanut chips and mini chocolate chips.

Set aside for a while.

Then, serve.

Enjoy.

8. Pearl Belgian Waffle

This is something exciting with love from Belgium!

Prep time: 07 minutes

Cooking time: 15 minutes

Servings: 1

Ingredients

- 1 pinch salt
- 1 cup milk
- 1 cup flour
- 1 teaspoon white sugar
- 1 pinch vanilla extract
- 1 tablespoon baking powder
- 4 tablespoons oil
- 1 cup halved mixed berries (blueberries and strawberry)
- 1 tablespoon syrup

Directions

Preheat the waffle iron to 255 degrees F.

Mix the dry ingredients in a bowl. Mix well.

Combine the wet ingredients except for the syrup in another bowl. Mix well.

Combine both mixtures.

IDA SMITH

Oil the grid before scooping the mixture in it.
Cook till you have exhausted your batter.
Transfer to a paper lined plate.
Add a drizzle of the syrup.
Enjoy.

9. Cinnamon Roll Waffle

Hmmmm!!! Delicious!!!?

Prep time: 06 minutes
Cooking time: 04 minutes
Servings: 2
Ingredients

- 1 cup milk
- 4 tablespoons butter
- 1 teaspoon baking powder
- 1 egg
- 1 teaspoon vanilla
- 1 cup flour
- 1 pinch salt
- 1 cup cream cheese topping

For the cinnamon topping

- 1 tablespoon cinnamon
- 2 tablespoons soft butter
- 2 tablespoons brown sugar

Directions

Heat the butter and milk in microwave safe bowl till the butter dissolves.

Transfer the mixture into a bowl. Add the vanilla and egg. Whisk well.

Add the salt, baking powder, and flour. Mix till nearly smooth.

Preheat your waffle maker.

Spoon the batter into the waffle maker. Cook till crispy.

Combine the cinnamon topping ingredients in a bowl. Mix well.

Serve the waffles. Garnish with a drizzle of the cream cheese topping and cinnamon topping.

Enjoy.

10. Strawberry Belgian Waffle

Do you want to learn how to prepare Belgian waffles from scratch and also explore your ingredients? This is the Belgian waffle recipe for you!!

Prep time: 06 minutes
Cooking time: 12 minutes
Servings: 8
Ingredients

- 4 eggs (separated the egg white and yolk)
- 4 tablespoons baking powder
- 8 tablespoons sugar
- 1 cup butter (melted)
- 4 cups flour
- 2 tablespoons cinnamon
- 1 pound strawberries (cut)
- 2 cups heavy whipped cream
- 3 teaspoons vanilla
- 1 pinch salt
- Whole strawberries for garnishing

Directions
Preheat the waffle iron to 255 degrees F.
Pulse half of the strawberries in the food processor.

Stir the egg yolks till peak.
Combine the egg whites, milk, flour, sugar, butter, cinnamon, salt, vanilla, and baking powder in a bowl. Mix well.
Add the egg yolk. Mix well.
Brush the iron with a little amount of butter.
Scoop the mixture on the waffle iron.
Cook till done.
Serve warm.
Add a drizzle of the strawberry puree on the waffles, followed by the whole strawberries and whipped cream.
Enjoy.

11. Belgian Red Tandoori Waffle

When India and Belgium decide to have a combo waffle, you should know it is going to be the bomb!!

Prep time: 09 minutes

Cooking time: 15 minutes

Servings: 4

Ingredients

- 1 tablespoon tandoori spices
- 80ml water
- 100g flour
- 30g sugar
- 80ml milk
- 2g dry yeast
- 40g butter
- 1 medium egg (separated)
- Strawberries and whipped cream to serve

Directions

Combine the butter, water, and milk in a pan. Cook till the liquid is warm and the butter dissolves.

Add the yeast and sugar. Cook-stir till the sugar dissolves.

Combine the flour and tandoori spices in a bowl. Add the egg yolk. Mix well before adding the warm milk mixture. Whisk well.

Whisk the egg white till peaks are formed.

Add to your batter.
Bake the waffles till you exhaust your batter.
Serve with strawberries and whipped cream.
Enjoy

12. Coconut Belgian Waffle

We agree that waffles are breakfast dishes, but what you don't know is that this Belgian recipe is much more than just your regular breakfast waffle! It is THE breakfast waffle that will give your day a lift!!

Prep time: 04 minutes
Cooking time: 06 minutes
Servings: 1
Ingredients

- 1 teaspoon coconut cream
- 3 tablespoons almond flour
- 1 small egg
- 1 dash xanthan gum
- 1 dash salt
- 1 teaspoon chives
- 1 dash onion powder
- 1 dash garlic powder
- 1 dash black pepper
- 1 tablespoon honey

Directions
Preheat the waffle iron.
Combine everything except for the honey in a big bowl. Mix well till your batter mixture is sticky and thick.

Brush the heated iron with oil.
Pour in half of the batter mixture in the lower grill of the iron.
Shut the grill and cook till the waffle is crispy and brown.
Transfer to a paper lined plate.
Pour in the remaining half of the batter mixture.
Cook as you did with the first half.
Transfer to a plate when it's brown and crispy. Serve and garnish with the honey.
Enjoy.

13. Blue Velvet Belgian Waffle

I remember when we said, "Let's try some blue waffles," and we laughed about it. We thought it wasn't a thing until we saw one in Belgium!!

Prep time: 09 minutes
Cooking time: 15 minutes
Servings: 2
Ingredients

- 1 cup flour
- 1 teaspoon baking powder
- 2 tablespoons granulated sugar
- 1 pinch baking soda
- 2 tablespoons cornstarch
- 1 pinch vanilla extract
- 1 tablespoon cocoa powder
- 1 pinch salt
- 1 cup buttermilk
- 1 big egg
- 1 teaspoon liquid blue food coloring
- 4 tablespoons oil

Directions
Preheat your waffle iron.
Combine the cornstarch, sugar, baking soda, flour, cocoa powder, baking powder, and salt in a bowl. Mix well.

Put the buttermilk, egg, food coloring, oil, and vanilla extract in a second bowl. Whisk to be well combined.
Stir in the flour mixture. Mix everything well.
Spray the iron with cooking spray.
Spoon the batter into the iron.
Cook till crispy.
Do the same with the remaining batter.
Serve.

14. Fairy Waffle Cookie

Rich in lots of sugar and butter, this old-fashioned Belgian waffle recipe is perfect for all your snack hangouts! It grants your waffle wishes just like a fairy!!!

Prep time: 05 minutes
Cooking time: 08 minutes
Servings: 30
Ingredients

- 3 eggs
- 2 cups flour
- 1 pinch baking powder
- 12 tablespoons sugar
- 14 tablespoons butter (melted)
- 1 dash salt
- 1 teaspoon vanilla extract

Directions
Preheat the waffle maker.
Combine the vanilla extract, baking powder, sugar, salt, and flour in a mixer. Mix well.
Break in the eggs one at a time.
Mix well.
Add the butter. Mix well.
Chill your batter for 40 minutes.

Scoop the batter in a ball form in the waffle maker.
Cook till done.
Serve.

15. Red Velvet and Chicken Belgian Waffle

Chicken and waffles? We bet that you didn't see those coming!!

Prep time: 07 minutes

Cooking time: 15 minutes

Servings: 3

Ingredients

- 1 medium egg
- 2 cups waffle mix
- 1 tablespoon red food coloring
- 1 teaspoon cocoa powder
- 1 teaspoon vanilla extract
- 6 chicken wings
- 1 cup coconut oil for frying
- 1 cup flour
- 1 cup mixed spices (black pepper, paprika, garlic powder, salt, and onion powder)

Directions

Season the chicken wings with the flour and mixed spices. Coat well.

Fry the coated chicken wings till crunchy.

Transfer to a plate.

Mix the waffle mix as instructed on the package. Then, stir in the cocoa powder, red food coloring, vanilla extract, and egg. Mix well.

Prepare the waffles till done.

Serve the waffles with the chicken wings.

16. Chocolate Belgian Waffle

Have you ever had waffles in a chocolate version? We bet you have not!

Try it out, will you?

You'd love every taste!!!

Prep time: 06 minutes

Cooking time: 08 minutes

Servings: 2

Ingredients

- 4 tablespoons flour
- 2 tablespoons cornstarch
- 2 tablespoons unsweetened cocoa
- 1 dash baking powder
- 1 dash baking soda
- 8 tablespoons buttermilk
- 1 dash salt
- 3 tablespoons soft butter
- 4 tablespoons sugar
- 8 tablespoons semi-sweet chocolate chips (crumbled)
- 1 teaspoon chocolate extract
- 1 medium egg (separated egg white chd yolk)
- 1 pinch espresso powder

Directions
Preheat the waffle iron.
Whisk the egg white till peaks form.
Mix the espresso powder, flour, chocolate chips, baking powder, cornstarch, cocoa, baking soda, and salt in a bowl.
Mix well.
Combine the milk, chocolate extract, sugar, egg yolk, and butter. Mix well.
Toss the dry and wet ingredients together. Mix well till well combined.
Add the egg white.
Keep the batter aside for 20 minutes.
Cook the waffles as instructed on your waffle iron.
Transfer to plates.
Serve immediately.

17. Banana Nutella Belgian Waffle

This Belgian Banana Nutella waffle would rock your waffle world!!

Prep time: 06 minutes

Cooking time: 10 minutes

Servings: 4

Ingredients

- 1 cup Nutella
- 2 medium eggs
- 2 medium bananas (mashed)
- 3 tablespoons oil
- 12 tablespoons milk
- 1 teaspoon vanilla extract
- 1 dash nutmeg
- 2 cups flour
- 1 teaspoon baking powder
- 1 dash salt
- 1 dash baking soda
- 3 teaspoons sugar
- 1 dash ground cinnamon
- Banana slices and whipped cream for topping

Directions

Combine the sugar, baking soda, baking powder, salt, flour, nutmeg, and cinnamon in a bowl. Mix well.

Combine the oil, eggs, milk, bananas, and vanilla extract in another bowl. Mix well.

Stir in the dry ingredients into the bowl of the wet ingredients. Whisk everything well.

Prepare the waffles as directed by the iron manufacturer.

Serve them. Add a drizzle of the Nutella. Top with banana slices and whipped cream.

18. Duck Confit and Belgian Waffle

A duck and waffle combo? We bet you didn't see this coming!! We didn't too at first!!!

Prep time: 15 minutes
Cooking time: 20 minutes
Servings: 3
Ingredients

- 1 garlic clove
- 2 tablespoons butter (melted)
- 1 store bought waffle (cubed)
- 1 teaspoon maple syrup
- 1 yellow onion (chopped)
- 1 teaspoon sage leaves (chopped)
- 1 medium carrot (diced)
- 2 dried apricots (chopped)
- 1 cup chicken broth
- 3 oz duck confit leg (shredded)
- 1 celery stalk (diced)
- 1 tablespoon pepper
- 1 pinch salt

Directions

Preheat the oven to 350 degrees F.
Arrange the waffle on a baking sheet.
Bake till crispy.
Put the butter in a pan and toss in the carrot, garlic clove, celery stalk, and onion.
Toss for 8 minutes.
Add a splash of the broth, the confit leg, apricots, pepper, salt, and sage leaves.
Cook for 3 minutes before adding the remaining broth, waffle, and syrup.
Pour the mixture into a casserole dish.
Bake till crispy.
Serve.

19. Liege Belgian Waffle

Either served warm or cooled, this Belgian waffle will melt your heart!!

Prep time: 08 minutes

Cooking time: 15 minutes

Servings: 3

Ingredients

- 2 medium eggs (separated)
- 6 tablespoons lukewarm milk
- 1 dash dry yeast
- 8 tablespoons butter (melted)
- 2 teaspoons white sugar
- 1 cup flour
- 9 tablespoons pearl sugar
- 1 dash salt
- 1 pinch vanilla extract

Directions

Preheat your waffle iron.

Add a sprinkle of the white sugar and yeast over the warm milk.

Keep aside for 10 minutes till the mixture becomes creamy.

Combine the butter, vanilla extract, yeast mixture, and eggs in a bowl. Mix well.

Add the salt and flour to another bowl. Mix well and form a well in the center of the bowl.

Pour in the butter mixture. Stir everything together. Cover and place the bowl in a warm place.
Scoop a ball size of the batter into the iron. Cook till crispy gold.
Do the same for the remaining batter.
Serve warm. Enjoy.

20. Whole Wheat Belgian Waffle

Are you tired of the regular flour? Or are you on a diet and want to prepare extra fiber waffles for you and your family? Don't sweat it; this whole grain waffle recipe is your best bet!!

Prep time: 10 minutes
Cooking time: 05 minutes
Servings: 1
Ingredients

- 1 pinch salt
- 1 teaspoon baking powder
- 1 medium egg
- 25g butter (melted)
- 33g wheat flour
- 110g milk
- 1 tablespoon granulated sugar

Directions
Preheat your waffle iron.
Combine the sugar, flour, and other dry ingredients in a bowl. Mix well.
Combine the butter, milk, and egg in another bowl. Mix well
Add both wet and dry ingredients together.
Bake the batter as instructed by your waffle iron.

Enjoy.

21. Nut Butter Belgian Waffle

Looking for an excuse to get nutty with your waffle? This Belgian recipe is saying, "Say no more, I get this!!"

Prep time: 08 minutes

Cooking time: 10 minutes

Servings: 2

Ingredients

- 1 egg (separated)
- 1 cup walnuts (chopped)
- 1 cup milk
- 8 tablespoons flour
- 1 tablespoon baking powder
- 8 tablespoons butter (melted)
- Walnuts and honey to serve

Directions

Preheat your waffle iron.

Grease with butter.

Whisk the egg white till stiff peaks are formed.

Combine the milk, flour, baking powder, butter, and egg yolk in a bowl. Mix well.

Add the walnuts and egg white.

Mix well.

Scoop the batter into the iron. Cook as directed by the iron manufacturer.
Serve warm with extra walnuts and honey.
Enjoy.

22. Sour Cream Belgian Waffle

Do you want to explore different waffle toppings, and you don't know the perfect waffle that would blend well with any waffle topping?

Why not try this sour cream Belgian waffle recipe out?

Prep time: 10 minutes

Cooking time: 10 minutes

Servings: 2

Ingredients

- 1 tablespoon sugar
- 2 tablespoons butter (melted)
- 8 tablespoons flour
- 1 teaspoon baking powder
- 1 egg
- 6 tablespoons sour cream
- 1 pinch vanilla extract
- 6 tablespoons milk

Directions

Preheat your waffle maker. Combine the wet ingredients first in a bowl. Whisk well.

Stir in the dry ingredients slowly.

Scoop the mixture into your waffle maker to make 2 large round waffles.

Serve warm.
Enjoy.

23. Double Chocolate Belgian Waffle

This is chocolatey deliciousness that you'd love!!

Prep time: 10 minutes
Cooking time: 20 minutes
Servings: 3
Ingredients

- 1 cup flour
- 1 pinch baking soda
- 1 tablespoon baking powder
- 1 tablespoon cornmeal
- 5 tablespoons cocoa powder
- 1 pinch salt
- 1 cup buttermilk
- 1 teaspoon vanilla
- 4 tablespoons chocolate chips
- 3 tablespoons coconut oil
- 1 large egg
- 1 pinch ground cinnamon
- 4 tablespoons granulated sugar
- 3 tablespoons whipped cream
- 2 tablespoons chocolate syrup

Directions
Combine the flour, cocoa powder, cornmeal, baking powder, sugar, baking soda, cinnamon, and salt in a bowl. Mix well.
Combine the wet ingredients in another bowl. Whisk well.
Stir the dry ingredients into the wet ingredient bowl. Mix well.
Add the chocolate chips.
Scoop the mixture into the waffle maker and cook as instructed on the maker.
Serve warm and garnish with the whipped cream, chocolate chips, and chocolate syrup.
Enjoy.

24. Red Cinnamon Belgian Waffle Cookie

Winter afternoons can get very boring when you're stuck up indoors because of the snow. Want to know how to make it better? Make some red cinnamon Belgian waffle cookies!!!

You'd love the experience!!!

Prep time: 15 minutes

Cooking time: 20 minutes

Servings: 40

Ingredients

- 3 cups flour
- 1 tablespoon vanilla extract
- 1 cup sugar
- 4 eggs
- 1 cup butter
- 2 tablespoons cinnamon
- 40 drops red food coloring
- 1 dash salt
- Any hot beverage to serve

Directions

Preheat your waffle iron.

Mix all your ingredients in a bowl.

Drop a spoonful of your batter right in the middle of your iron where the four portions are joined.

Shut your iron and cook the waffle.
Do till the batter is exhausted.
Serve immediately with any hot beverage!!

25. Nutella Belgian Waffle

This decadent Nutella filled waffle will have you smacking your lips afterwards!!

Prep time: 08 minutes

Cooking time: 09 minutes

Servings: 2

Ingredients

- 4 tablespoons Nutella
- 2 cups honey biscuit dough

Directions

Preheat the iron.

Grease with oil or butter.

Break the biscuit dough in half.

Make them flat into circles.

Scoop a spoonful of the Nutella on one dough circle in the center.

Cover with the other circle.

Put the sealed dough circles in the iron. Shut the iron.

Cook till all of the dough layers are cooked.

Microwave the remaining Nutella and drizzle in the waffles.

Serve.

26. Ice Cream Waffle Sandwich

If you have ever thought of waffles as a beautiful work of art, this recipe is a confirmation of your thought!!

Prep time: 25 minutes

Cooking time: 15 minutes

Servings: 2

Ingredients

- 8 tablespoons flour
- 1 pinch baking soda
- 1 handful blueberries
- 1 tablespoon oil
- 1 egg
- 8 tablespoons buttermilk
- 1 teaspoon baking powder
- 1 pinch salt

For the fillings and toppings

- 1 cup blueberry preserves
- 1 cup milk chocolate (melted)
- 1 cup white chocolate (melted)
- 1 handful toasted crushed peanuts
- 1 cup cooked bacon (crumbled)

- 2 cups vanilla ice cream

Directions
Preheat your waffle maker.
Put the first set of the ingredients in a large bowl.
Mix well.
Cook the waffles as indicated by your waffle maker.
Transfer the hot cooked waffles to a plate to cool.
Ensure they don't stick together.
When cool, cut them in half to form triangles.
Scoop the ice cream on top of each half of the waffles. Spread the ice cream out.
Add a scoop of the preserve on the ice cream. Spread it out too.
Place two halves of the waffles in each other. Chill till the ice cream gets hard.
Combine the melted chocolates in a bowl.
Put the bacon and peanuts on another plate.
Coat the chilled waffles in the bowl of the chocolates first and add a sprinkle of the peanuts and bacon to the coated waffles.
Chill the coated waffles for 2 hours.
Serve immediately.

27. Egg Fast Belgian Waffle

With just five ingredients, this low carb and gluten-free waffle recipe is yours to enjoy!!

Prep time: 07 minutes
Cooking time: 07 minutes
Servings: 2
Ingredients

- 1 pinch salt
- 4 eggs
- 1 tablespoon vanilla
- 2 tablespoons coconut oil
- 2 oz cream cheese

Directions
Preheat your waffle iron.
Combine everything in the food processor. Process till smooth.
Spoon into your iron.
Cook till the waffle is golden brown.
Do for the rest of the batter.
Serve.

28. Egg Less Belgian Waffle

What is a waffle without an egg? It's a delicious Belgian waffle!!! Have you ever tried making it?

You don't want to risk, right?!

But this egg-less Belgian waffle will blow your mind! Try it out!!

Prep time: 05 minutes

Cooking time: 08 minutes

Servings: 5

Ingredients

- 1 cup flour
- 1 tablespoon sugar
- 2 tablespoons baking powder
- 1 cup milk
- 1 tablespoon water
- 1 tablespoon oil
- 2 tablespoons butter (melted)
- 1 teaspoon vanilla extract

Directions

Preheat your waffle maker.

Mix the sugar, baking powder, and flour in a bowl. Mix well.

Combine the wet ingredients in another bowl. Mix well.

Toss both ingredients together. Whisk well to get a slightly lumpy batter.
Spoon the batter into the waffle maker. Cook till the waffles are done. Do for the rest of the batter.
Serve immediately.

29. Belgian Chaffle

If you are wondering what "Chaffle" means, it simply means cheese and egg waffle!! Sounds cool, right?! Of course!!!

Prep time: 05 minutes
Cooking time: 04 minutes
Servings: 2
Ingredients

- 8 tablespoons Cheddar cheese (shredded)
- 1 large egg
- Syrup for garnishing

Directions
Preheat your waffle iron.
Combine the egg and cheese in a bowl. Mix well.
Brush the iron with butter.
Spoon the batter in the iron. Shut the iron and cook till golden crispy.
Do the same to your remaining batter.
Serve and garnish with syrup.
Enjoy.

30. Belgian Waffle Benedict and Tomatoes

If you are a lover of Eggs Benedicts and waffles, there is no reason why you can't have a combo of both!!

Who says you can't?! Definitely not us!!

Prep time: 08 minutes

Cooking time: 12 minutes

Servings: 2

Ingredients

- 1 cup hollandaise sauce
- 1 cup roasted tomatoes (sliced)
- 130g flour
- 1 tablespoon sugar
- 1 teaspoon baking powder
- 180g milk
- 2 medium eggs (separated)
- 1 pinch salt
- 4 tablespoons butter (melted)
- 2 eggs

Directions

Preheat your waffle iron.

Combine the baking powder, sugar, salt, and flour in a bowl. Mix well.

Mix the egg yolks, butter, and milk in another bowl. Whisk well.

Whisk the egg whites till peaks form.

Add the egg whites to the flour mixture. Add the butter mixture slowly.

Spray the heated iron with cooking spray. Scoop the batter into the iron.

Cook till done. Transfer to a plate.

Fry the eggs as an omelet. Set aside.

Lay the waffles on plates. Add the tomatoes to the waffles, followed by the omelet.

Add a drizzling of the hollandaise sauce.

Serve.

Conclusion

Wow! Wow!! Wow!!

If you had thought that there was just one way to prepare waffles, this Belgian waffle cookbook has shown you beyond reasonable doubts that you can prepare waffles in tons of ways!

So, what are you going to do next?

That is exactly what you are thinking!!

Get your ingredients and start making diverse and delicious waffles, courtesy of the Belgian waffle cookbook!!

Till I see you again in my next cookbook, Go Waffles!!!!

Don't miss out!

Visit the website below and you can sign up to receive emails whenever Ida Smith publishes a new book. There's no charge and no obligation.

https://books2read.com/r/B-A-LRXL-ARYRB

BOOKS 2 READ

Connecting independent readers to independent writers.

www.ingramcontent.com/pod-product-compliance
Lightning Source LLC
Chambersburg PA
CBHW060613120726
48002CB00010B/2950